How To Achieve Your Highest Potential

7 Secrets to A Successful Career

By

Dr. Gregory Haughton

ISBN-13: 978-1518781513
ISBN-10: 1518781519

About the Author

Dr. Gregory Orlando Haughton is a three time Olympic Medalist who won the World Championship, Goodwill Games Championship, and Pan American Games Championship. He received his Ph.D. in Business management from North Central University.

He utilizes his vast athletic and academic experience and knowledge to assist individuals in achieving their highest career potential. He has experienced the joys of being on top and the frustrations of when one fails to achieve a career goal. He understands that adversity can bring out the best in people; however, he also believes that experience is not always the best teacher.

His experiences have taught him that the path to achieving success is a formidable one without the right support and guidance to deal with many of life's challenges. His experiences of growing up in the inner city, taught him how to convert negative circumstances into motivational catalysts to overcome them.

The most defining personal moments of his life are: receiving an athletic scholarship to the Central Arizona, becoming a three time Olympic Medalists, overcoming personal odds of receiving his Ph.D. after his wife died leaving him to raise their daughters.

He is enthusiastic about sharing his philosophy and athletic accomplishments while teaching his success principles to those who desire athletic advice and professional guidance in their sports and life. He inspires you to achieve your highest career potential by tapping into the reservoir of your mind to retrieve the truth that lies within you.

He develops individuals to become emotionally and psychologically aware in order to deal with life's challenges, along with intentional actions that manifest positive results.

He strongly believes that with hard work and the right guidance, you will recognize the true leader within; but you must first liberate yourself from old realities or justifications that prevent you from achieving your highest potential.

His philosophy has helped him to make a positive difference in the lives of many people. He knows that successful individuals rarely make it on their own; they succeed because they enlist the help and experience of individuals who can lead, guide, counsel, motivate and provide key techniques, and strategies. He has established the Haughton Mentoring group whose vision is to inspire individuals to achieve their highest potential in their career.

What Career People Are Saying

"This book is very informative and will have a positive impact on career individuals lives and professional career. This book not only contains fascinating insights on how to advance one career, but it also imparts strategies to cope with pressures from managers when working in a stressful environment."

Professor Claudette Lawrence
Business Professor

"This book provides the knowledge and guidance that young career individuals need in order to advance in their career. If your goal is to be successful in your career, this is the book for you. It is packed with professional advice on what it takes to succeed in a high demanding profession. These insights and strategies will have an immediate impact on your career performance."

Felicia Meadow
Law Professor and Practicing Attorney

"As a professional manager, it is your personality that determines whether you are liked by your subordinates. This book provide strategies to help career individuals understand the importance of having the right personality, dedication and focus that influence career success.

This book will propel you to stay committed to your goal even when all is appear lost. If it's your desire to be successful, this book can make the difference."

-Richard Gayle:
Finance Manager/Portfolio management
& Brokerage/Wealth management

Acknowledgments

We would like to extend our special thanks to all of our immediate family and friends, the important people who have assisted me in reaching my highest potential in life.

Special thanks to my late wife Simone Haughton who stood by my side and believed in my abilities to write this book. Her inspiration, love, affection, wisdom, knowledge, and guidance made it easy to formulate, plan and conduct my research interviews. Simone, you will forever be that beacon of light that guide my daily thoughts and actions. You will forever be missed.

Special thanks to Louis McDonald, who has been my conscience and go to person in time of need, work and business. Your friendship and kindness will forever be appreciated.

Thanks to Lorraine Robinson who continues to guide my action during challenging and lonely times. Your love and kindness has no bounds.

Thanks to my brothers and friends Milton Murphy, Cory Lewis, Curtis Cornwall, Allan Haye, Dr. Doyen Williams, Chris Abrahams, Victor Greenland, Shauna Smith and Dr. Harold Davis for your time, energy, love and support. I will forever love you all for being my friends and guides to the end. May God continue to bless and keep you safe!

Dr. Gregory Haughton

Table of Contents

Chapter 1
Introduction

What Are Your Career Goals?

Do you set realistic goals for yourself? How do you know if your goals are achievable? Do you set goals using your emotional and physical senses? Your desired goal should be to improve incrementally, while staying stress free, and enjoying life. To achieve your highest potential in your life, be willing to incrementally implement a philosophy and strategy that is designed to develop and integrate your knowledge and experience, both physically and mentally.

Moving up the chain of command is not achieved through inspiration alone; it is achieved through integration where mind and body are in sync and you follow through with the right action. To improve your performance and achieve your highest potential in life and career, use a proven and reliable philosophy to guide your decision making process.

The most successful people in an organization are not the hardest workers; they are the fully integrated who use strategies to leverage and delegate when necessary.
By now, you may understand that only a proven philosophy will have the power to assist you in achieving your highest potential quickly.

Highest Potential

"Highest Potential" is your ability to perform at your best at any moment within your individual and respective activity. It is the blueprint and bedrock from which you build your career performance and advancement." Many career individuals begin to advance in their career with hard work, only to realize that without proper guidance hard work alone is still not enough to achieve a satisfying career. Therefore, individuals who lack the needed counsel and support from an experienced mentor may become discouraged, frustrated and disgusted with their position in life, which oftentimes leads to even more pitfalls that restrict personal growth. By accepting leadership from a person who has been down that path before you can learn how to challenge yourself mentally and psychologically. Therefore, know how to be triumphant over a system that does not have your best interests at heart.

Never forget, to revisit and analyze your "Highest Potential" frequently if you expect to have full knowledge and control over your thoughts, mind and actions. This book will provide you with cutting edge information and inspiration to gain many insights to allow you to make any necessary adjustments to reach your full career potential. Being in tune with your goals is essential to your career success. You, more than anyone else should know and believe in what you do and why you are doing it.

What Can This Book Do For You?

This manual is the key and guide to achieving your highest career potential - guaranteed. If the information in this book is applied properly, it will assist you to develop into a better-rounded person with the ability to control your thoughts, emotions and decision making competencies like never before. Every concept in this book is fundamental to the art of achieving career success. It will guide you to work smarter, without having to worry about burnouts, which normally restrict your advancement in your career. As you read through the information in this book, you will see just how easy it is to achieve your highest career potential quickly.

As a Three Time Olympic Medalist and World Champion, I enjoy this opportunity to use my experience and knowledge to assist you in achieving your highest potential. I know the frustration that comes when one fails to reach a desired goal. I also have experienced the joy of reaching my dreams and understand what it takes to get there athletically. The same principles I used in my career have easily transferred into my career and then my business. My mission is to assist career individuals who have a strong desire to achieve their highest potential, but aren't quite sure how to get there or have had disappointments in their current career position, and is seeking a better way.

This book will provide the motivation and encouragement to those career individuals who seek career advancement immediately. It will also help the reader to recognize the true power within.

I firmly believe that you too can, and will, reach your highest potential in your career with the help of my philosophy as discussed in this book: but you must first make the choice to be committed to applying these success principles that I teach.

80% of your success is mental, and 20% is performing the right activities. Without the right mental preparation you will not have the ability to see through all the illusions you encounter in life.

With the right mental preparation you will be able to decide what you really want to experience, and then take the proper actions to manifest your dreams.

As the founder of my group, the Haughton Mentoring Group Inc. (HMG), I promise to do everything in my power to help you achieve your career success. If you're not successful, I'm not successful.

My reputation depends on your success! Let's get started today to develop and bring out the winner in you.

Working Smarter is the Solution

Wisdom is present in all instances where success is found. Success requires using the right mental and physical principles to accomplish your goals. Working harder is not the complete solution; however, doing the right mental and physical activities smarter is the key to achieving your career and personal success.

In my personal endeavors, it is only when I embraced the correct mental and physical principles that I became more in tune with my body and mind. I grew wiser, stronger, faster, and had a better understanding about who I wanted to be and what my purpose was in my sport. I have been able to transfer this knowledge to my career, business and personal life. You can accomplish the same thing in your career and personal life.

What You Don't Know Will Limit Your Growth

When we refuse to acknowledge that we don't know what we don't know, we not only ignore the warning signs but we may not even be aware of them. At other times we let our own stubbornness or false pride get in the way.

I must admit, when I was in that state of mind of when I thought I knew everything, I was unaware that many of the thoughts and words I used to motivate myself and identify my purpose to achieve my goals were low in energy (fear, shame, pride, guilt, grief and anger) and as a result, my energy and level of consciousness were low.

In other words, when a person's energy level and consciousness is low, they are more likely to have a false sense of reality. This false sense of reality may influence you to do and say things that are not in your best interest.

Believe me it is not in your best interest to pretend you know all the answers. Deep down you know that you need help because you are not getting the desired results. If you are not getting your desired results, you need help, period.

For instance, some of the most successful athletes such as Michael Jordon, Wayne Gretzky, Walter Payton, Derek Jeter, Tiger Woods, and Usain Bolt all not only received help but knew they needed help from experienced coaches, personal trainers and nutritionists in order to perform at their highest potential throughout their careers. Do not attempt to take on this challenge on your own because it is a difficult task to accomplish without the right knowledge, guidance and support! There is a premise that states: If it is possible for one person then it is possible for another. The only question then is how?

This may be your only chance to receive guidance and proper advice on what to do, what to say, how to think and how to act. The missing ingredient for most people is the support and proper guidance to assist them in thinking the right thoughts and taking the proper action which will result in the desired outcome.

Dr. Gregory Haughton

Chapter 2
Overcoming Self-Doubt, Poor Self-Discipline

"Everyone needs time to grow. Those who have the discipline to use their time wisely will achieve their highest potential quicker than those who don't."– Dr. Greg Haughton

The fundamental problems that limit the average employee from advancing in their career are self-doubt, poor self-discipline and lack of understanding as to what is expected of them to advance. The person may be a dedicated worker, but they may lack the knowledge and discipline to continue doing the right activities. When such disciplines are lacked, the person may also lose control of their thoughts and feelings, which oftentimes limits their personal and career growth.

Knowing how and when to seek guidance in order to advance and grow in an organization can be difficult if the employee is unaware that they need guidance let alone the type of guidance required to be successful. However, it is important to know that the power to advance in a career is a result of seeking the guidance of others who are successful in their respective line of work. Remove the limitations from your mind and apply the techniques in this book. This will improve your level of consciousness and provide direction to assist you as you excel in your career.

All of us can learn to remove mental limitations. With renewed confidence, you will learn how to work smart by becoming mentally aware of your true conceptual power and inner strength that lies within you. If you learn to master these tasks, your success will be imminent and your managers and co-workers will grow to appreciate and respect you.

Why Sacrifice Growth for Short Term Gains.

What if I told you that most people tend to sacrifice their long term success and future for short term gratification? Success is possible to every person regardless of their circumstances.

However, because many of us were not taught strategies on how to align our thoughts with the required action we are not able to think outside our limited defined box.

In order to discover and achieve success, tap into a proven system that is designed to elevate your level of awareness. Only by embracing the right knowledge with experience can you achieve your highest potential in your career and personal life.

Trial & Error Limits Your Career Growth

Discipline weighs ounces, and regret weighs tons. You do not want to experience the weight of regret, so start by doing the things that will enhance your chances to achieve your career success.

You can then create a strategy that will assist you in achieving your highest potential, if necessary, with the help of a mentor.

A mentor's guidance possess insights and foresights not visible to you in your current situation. A mentor with similar life experiences should be one of the first cornerstones on your new path towards achieving success.

If you ask the most successful people in their established careers what it takes to achieve their highest potential, the answer would be amazingly simple: Your success is not the result of having a "hoping" or "wishing" attitude toward your goals and dreams – it is the discipline to maintain the right mental and physical activities day in – day out.

Additionally, associating yourself with a proven mentor will allow you to tap into the proper discipline for success.

Finding the Inspiration From Within

Since you are reading this book I assume you are highly inspired to be successful in your life; as such, it should be easy to maintain your inspiration and bring excitement and enthusiasm to your career and life.

Proper mental and physical harmony is required throughout your life; therefore be open to receive and willing to apply the appropriate knowledge and wisdom required for your career and life situations. Remember, your natural talent alone will not fully benefit you if you do not make the right choices regardless of your circumstances. As such, be forthcoming and be completely honest with yourself with regards to your current abilities and attributes that may be sabotaging your progress.

The Right Mental Perspective increases Success

In dealing with career individuals, one of the most common mistakes is their tendency to bypass the information, knowledge and principles that build a solid foundation. Instead, they engage in activities that are counterproductive to their long term growth and potential. The problem with that is, they are unaware or unable to predict the cause and effect consequences of their decisions.

Many things can be used to help you achieve your highest career potential, but they only make a difference if you already have a solid foundation of the correct information with the know how to support it.
Imagine trying to build a 60 story sky scraper without a solid foundation; even if you managed to get a few floors up, it would eventually collapse.

Many career individuals have had their careers prematurely ended because they did not have the important foundational knowledge to begin with. It breaks my heart that a person can be taught how to do a routine task without ever being taught the basic knowledge of the cause and effect or the consequences of their decisions, whether those are deemed good or bad.

The right mindset and knowledge are important in your career in order to survive in a world that is constantly changing and is becoming more competitive.

Investing in your education is absolutely essential and should never be overlooked. If you intend to perform at a high level in your career then you need to study consistently, rest, eat a balanced meal, and re-hydrate yourself.

Believe it or not, these are important. The right education and knowledge will guide you in these areas, but it starts with nailing down the basics first.

Don't make the mistake of going straight into performing an activity without knowing the short and long term consequences of your decision. If you skip this step, your hard work and dedication may help very little or not at all towards your career will advancement and you find yourself discouraged with your career aspirations sooner than you can imagine.

Dr. Gregory Haughton

Chapter 3
Commit to Doing the Right Activities

Dr. Gregory Haughton said, *"Success begins in the mind. Before success is manifested in reality, it is conceived in the mind first. So is courage."*

The first secret to achieve your highest career potential is to decide and intend in your heart and mind to do whatever it takes to ensure your career advancement. Your primary objective is to channel and focus your mental energy on controlling your thoughts. Your ability to control your thoughts and feelings help you commit to your plan of action even when things are not going your way.

Most career individuals who fail to achieve their highest career potential have it backwards. They believe that the motivation and desire to achieve their career potential is by having a strong desire to do the activities they enjoy the most. This is not true.

In fact, most successful career individuals do not work because they enjoy working. They chose to push themselves because they enjoy the internal gratification that comes from their efforts. To achieve your highest career potential means that you do the things you do not want to do in order to achieve the things you want to enjoy.

If you are struggling to achieve your highest career potential, then maybe it's time to reflect on your past actions to determine what your mental aptitude was when you made your career decisions as well as your personal decisions.

Having a successful career begins with making the mental commitment to fully invest in your mind, body and career. Partial investment in mind and body will only return partial or minimal results in your career. When you are mentally invested in your career advancement you will learn to develop the right mental attitude. In turn your mental judgement will guide and discourage you from participating in activities that are counterproductive to your career advancement.

With consistency and a determined mindset, you can quickly develop the discipline to realize your full career potential. Your commitment, motivation, along with the proper amount of physical and mental energy will be focused on doing the right tasks.

For instance, if it's your desire to someday become an expert in computer engineering, then you must first intend in your heart and mind that you will make the mental commitment to sacrifice all things that will become obstacles to your goal. Obstacles are guaranteed as they are the building blocks for the courage and stamina you will need in order to succeed.

The right mindset will push you to do the things that will make your dreams a reality. You must purpose in your heart that you will find the motivation and the will to study all you can about computer software, computer hardware and computer programming even when you lack the desire and drive to do so. Without the mindset and determination to invest your time and energy wisely your career dreams may never become a reality.

Even if you are mediocre in your technical abilities, with the right mental commitment you can easily outshine those individuals who are immensely talented, but choose not to invest wholeheartedly in their mental training.

Successful People invest in Mental Preparation

The reason people find it difficult to manifest the results they deserve is because they are not fully vested in what they are doing mentally. They work hard at ninety percent, instead of training their mind at one hundred percent. The remaining ten percent is never a physical push as much as a mental one.

Why do you think some people refuse to invest in the mental preparation for their long term future? When several Olympians were asked this question, they responded by saying, "At first we refused to integrate mental preparation as a part of our training because we did not know how important it was to our development."

Not investing in mental training for career individual has proven to be highly detrimental to their short and long term career future. The same outcome will manifest in your career if you refuse to invest mentally in your career future!

It's All in Mental Commitment

Your commitment to becoming a great CEO or manager may appear to be a physical commitment; however, in reality, your commitment will be a mental one. Before you can tap into your physical ability, first make the mental commitment to invest in your future, by reading personal self-development books, attending seminars and workshops, etc. If you refuse to first make the mental commitment prior to pursuing excellence, it is highly unlikely that you will achieve your highest potential. Individuals who refuse to make that mental commitment will find it difficult to succeed in whatever they decide on doing and becoming.

Become Mentally Entrusted in Your Career

The plan to achieve career success is never just mental – the plan is physical as well. The plan provides the overall structure for the way you want things to progress overtime. It should not be set in stone – as changes will occur you should be able to adapt or make adjustments in order for you to achieve your career goals.

Sometimes the plan requires drastic changes, and other times minor cosmetic adjustments are necessary based on the different sets of circumstances.

The **Greg Haughton Overload Concept** supports the theory that if you force your mind to do things and process new information, over time, your ability to use positive Creative Energy will allow the body to adapt and handle the new activity more efficiently, and this will increase your mental ability, to handle the increased workload.

The body and mind will become stronger over time and will become highly capable to supply the necessary motivation to complete the tasks. This will pay great dividends in the future.

The Laws of Success

These laws can work for us or against us, but they are the secret that will allow you to achieve your highest potential in all areas of your life.

These laws work through us if we follow them, or work against us if we ignore them. Several years ago I had the pleasure to discuss this topic with several CEOs, Olympians and world champion athletes. They were asked, "What were the major differences in your thought process when you were successful in your career compared to when you thought you failed?" They all agreed that their negative thoughts were destructive to their confidence, beliefs, work ethics, decision making and judgments which resulted in initial failures.

These CEOs and world class athletes confirmed that such thoughts produce frustrations which were the principal cause of their poor decision making, and therefore resulted in unfulfilled desires.

These results began as negative thoughts which then manifested in their personality and behavior. No one can escape this law of positive thinking. Understanding how these laws work will make a significant difference in your career and personal life.

We do not create these laws that govern our behaviors; we discover them in the course of studies, interaction with others and when life circumstances cause us to question our feeble or disastrous results.

We sometimes infer that luck plays a significant role in the process that leads us to discover and then implement these laws. However, these laws do not play favorites; it is not about being lucky in our career and life. The laws are revealed to us when we are ready for them and then the right teacher will appear or we are finally open to discover them and then implement them. We are all governed by the same laws and principles.

To achieve your Highest Potential in your career, use the laws and principles and allow them to work through you, around you, and from you.

Talent alone does Not Ensure Career Success.

Studies support that talent alone does not guarantee a person career success. Why? Because success is not determine by a person's talent; it is determine by the person's mental and physical commitment to doing a particular activity. For instance, if two individuals with equivalent talents are prepared to equally invest in doing the right activities, then both can achieve similar career success.

However, if one of them chooses to invest more time and effort in additional self-developmental activities such as, reading of books, watching videos, attending seminars and workshops in his/her field, that person will substantially increase their chances to achieve their success. The person who chooses not to invest in these activities may find success formidable especially during challenging times.

Investing in the right mental training is deemed successful because it can help to guide a person perspective, actions and behaviors. It also provides the confidence and inspiration to find the determination to overcome challenges especially during thought-provoking circumstances.

Success is not a respecter of person; success is influenced by your commitment and determination to doing the right mental and physical activities. In fact, success does not care if you are conscious of what the right activities are, as long as it is done.   For that reason, knowing what the right activities are, and then doing them relentlessly have always assured my success.

Sometimes we are aware of the right activities, but we may lack the desire to do them. When individuals with promising potential underachieve in their respective career, it affects their psychological and emotional well-being; it also affects their respective teams, family, and friends. Unfortunately, without adequate mentors to help you cope with your self-imposed pressures, limitations and other forms of personal challenges you will continue to struggle to achieve your career and personal goals.

Total Commitment of Body & Mind

When I was 16 years old, I was able to achieve some of my potential of my God given talent.   However, at age 26, I realized that getting by on talent alone was not enough. In order to dominate in my sport, I had to totally commit my mind and body in order to achieve my purpose.

I became aware that I needed to understand the reason behind performing an activity. Once I understood I was then committed to the process. When I was prepared, I trusted that the preparation would be sufficient to help me perform at my highest potential.

When I was at the Olympics Games and other major sporting events, my focus was never on winning. My focus was on competing to the best of my ability.   I managed my thoughts to such an extent that it led to the correct actions to bring about my desired results.   I was prepared to do exactly the things that my training put me in the position to do.   If that was done, the result was satisfactory.

Additionally, you want to be prepared enough to be able to trust that you can overcome any situation you may encounter, correctly assess the situation and then make the necessary adjustments to get your desired results. Winning is never guaranteed, but doing your best should be the focus in all you do.

For instance, there have been occasions where I had achieved my highest potential, but still lost the race because someone performed better than I did on that day. However, if I gave my best effort on that particular day, I was happy with my performance. With that mental practice in place, I was prepared to continue my training and move on to the next race/event in my life. Never focus on winning as the ultimate outcome; winning is not guaranteed. Why?

There are too many variables to winning that are beyond your control; however, be prepared to do your best on and off the job, and trust that you are equipped to execute your strategy.

Your best is adjusted to the uncontrolled variables or circumstances. For example, your best is completely different when you are not feeling well or may have some injury. As said before it is not always about achieving the outcome you desire. If at the end of the day you can be satisfied that you gave it your best effort, that itself is reward enough. As long as you keep focused on that – always doing your best, you will achieve your highest potential.

Never forget that deep and lasting career success comes from making the mental decision to purpose in your heart to do whatever it takes to achieve your highest career potential. By making the mental decision to change the way you think about your career plans, along with your level of commitment to doing the right activities, you are now able to tap into your inner self with confidence and maximize your true potential in your career.

Chapter 4
7 Laws to Achieve Career Success

"To achieve your highest potential you will have to travel many intricate terrains. Prepare yourself for traveling this journey by doing the right mental and physical activities; this makes the journey less challenging." – Dr. Gregory Haughton

The secret to having a great career and personal life is not found in the top of your organizations', nor in their business philosophy or strategies. Reason being is that their interest is diametrically opposite yours in that they are only interested in how you can help them advance their own career and the company's bottom line.

Do not depend on your organization to educate you in order to bring them more value. Take the initiative to educate yourself and then bring more value to your company. We have witnessed many careers and personal failures over the years. You and only you are responsible for what happens in your career or life.

According to Dr. Harold Davis, these seven laws should be used to guide our aspirations in life and our career goals. If you fail to obey and follow these laws in your career and life your failure is imminent.

Law #1 Law of Pure Potentiality

According to Dr. Davis, the law of pure potential suggests that you have all the potential within you to achieve your desires if you are willing to do the right activities that it requires.

The key to your career success is to realize and tap into the unlimited potential of this power **by identifying with it, and having faith in it.** This will allow you to adequately prepare yourself for the real world experiences that you will encounter. Get on the side of the Universe if you desire to benefit from its full power.

Law #2 Law of Intention

The Law of Intention requires that you have a true intent to accomplish what you say you want to accomplish in your career. Do you get motivated sometimes only to find out later during challenging times that you do not have the true desire to do what it takes to achieve your potential?

Without a true desire to achieve success, this law will not work for you. It's not a question of merely having a wanting or hopeful attitude towards the Creative Energy in order for it to work for you. This principle is about making a solid commitment to experience the desired results with the power of your words, thoughts and feelings. It is through intention that you plant the right seeds for your success. When all conditions for your success have been planted for an amazing career, it will happen spontaneously without much effort. Release all negative words, thoughts, feelings and persons from your life and you will find the true intent to achieve your highest potential!

Law #3 Law of Cause and Effect

This is one of the most important laws. According to Dr. Davis, if you speak, think, and feel the right thoughts, you will manifest the right results. It is impossible for you to think of a bad career experience and then manifest a great career. These are diametrically opposing thoughts, aren't they?

I realized later in my career that all good and bad performances started in my mind first. As a result, I try my best to start my day with the right thoughts and feelings. These practices have continued to have a positive effect on my attitude, and greatly influence my ability to perform successfully.

My athletic performance was great when I followed my empowered thoughts and feelings. It's just like the farmer who plants a row of carrot seeds. What does he expect to harvest in approximately eighty days? Carrots, of course! The day a farmer's carrot seeds produce watermelons will be the day when something awry is taking place in the Universe.

Law #4 Law of Giving and Receiving

This law creates the flow in all successes. If you give willingly and freely to and of yourself, you will manifest the same in return. To be successful in your career, focus on how you can give your best. Help your coworkers achieve their best whenever you can; be supportive to your company's vision and mission and everything associated with it.

Whatever you want to experience in your career and life, you must first give it. The more of it you give, the more you will receive in return. Giving starts the abundant flow of the Creative Energy in your career and life. Your words, thoughts and feelings will create the pattern for its creation.

Throughout my competitive career I gave advice to my competitors without reservation. I realized that the more I gave to others, the easier it was for me to achieve my potential. When I gave more of myself to others, I received an abundance of help from others. The more time I contributed to building a solid foundation mentally, physically and spiritually, the better results I received.

Let me give you an example. When I was a sophomore in high school, the more time I gave to myself in the forms of denying myself of things that were detrimental to my career goals, the more I improved my performance in the 400m. For instance, in less than a year I improved my performance from 51:70 seconds to 46:88 seconds.

The next year, as a freshman in college, I improved my performance from 46:88 seconds to 44:78 seconds and became the second fastest Jamaican in the 400 meters.

The difference between my past and future success was the time spent in doing the right mental and physical activities. I realized that the more I gave of myself, the more I improved mentally and physically in my career performance.

Once I became conscious of my physical and mental potential, and the type of Creative Energy required achieving success, I invested more time and energy and included the appropriate Creative Energy to train potential.

Law #5 Law of Detachment

This law states that you trust the Universe. If you have adopted the right mental philosophy and career training pattern, based on the right principles, then you will produce the right results. Do not be concerned with the actual means of obtaining the results. It would be like a farmer digging up the seeds he planted the day before to check on their progress. This is counterproductive and demonstrates a grim lack of faith in your efforts and the program. If you continue to trust in your ability and strategy, then with time you will achieve your highest potential.

When I was competing at the Goodwill Games in Australia in 2001, I was in great physical shape and my mental condition was growing stronger each day. I realized that if I followed my race plan, I would achieve my highest potential based on my level of preparation; this improved my chances of having a successful competition. I won the competition by five meters, and I am certain it was the result of following my race plans to the best of my ability and not being attached to the outcome; in so doing, I ran my best race.

The goal is to achieve your highest potential, not your supervisor's or associates. Remember that your superiors have their own objectives that may not necessarily align with your objective.

Once your objective is clear and you have done your work of thinking and staying positive as well as doing the right activities, allow the Universe to take care of the details. This is the way for you to be the creative factor.

Remember, chances are, everyone is asking for Divine help, as if God would actually play favorites. However, we know this is not the case; the outcome will always be a result of your consciousness, as well as the quality of your mental and physical preparation.

Law#6 Law of Averages

Any activity performed consistently will yield a result that develops into a pattern of predictable results.

The operation of this law is evident when we observe the collective consciousness of the human race. This factor of the law of averages will normally result in about an eighty to twenty percent ratio, where twenty percent of people will do the work and achieve success while the other eight percent flounder around being a victim of circumstances.

You don't have to be susceptible to the effects of this law. You don't have to be average in your career. You do not need to settle in your career when the sky is the limit for you. You can rise above it by making a choice which is in harmony with the Creative Energy. This power to choose is within you.

Average results are illusions; however, choose to live outside of the options of being an average person and rise above this Law. Simply put, cast your vote based on what you believe, and what do you believe? – that you are amazing and powerful and will achieve your highest potential in all that you set out to do in life and career.

Be careful of the things you say and believe, because your false beliefs can quickly become disappointing reality.

While I attended college in Arizona, I believed that only a few athletes were truly special, and that only these few had the perfect mix of skills to become an elite competitor.

I must admit, I was blinded by the myth that great athletes are born and not developed.

It wasn't until I competed at the Sun Angel Classic in Arizona that I realized that I could be an elite athlete. This shattered my old beliefs and myths and allowed me to realize that I could rise above the averages.

Once I became conscious of this, my perception changed, as well as my approach to training and competing. With this revelation and rise in consciousness, I was able to elevate my thoughts above the law of averages. I was able to accomplish this by literally taking my vote out of the collective unconsciousness of the human race which perpetuates the law of averages.

You can take your vote out of the collective unconsciousness just by making the choice to do so; it requires direct action in order for you to start achieving your highest potential in your career and life. You do not need to think and act like the average person.

The average person's level of consciousness is low, and therefore they are more susceptible to be influenced by negative thoughts as well as by the actions of others.

When you decide to take your vote out of the collective unconsciousness, you have absolute power to use only the positive Creative Energy to influence your life and career.

Law #7 Law of Least Effort

This law describes your harmonious alignment with the Creative Energy. When you are so aligned, you leverage real power to yield results based on the lowest expenditure of personal energy. Real Power is energy that never depletes itself, so it would be wise to get on the side of the Universe.

According to Dr. Davis, to operate at your best, you must practice and use these Universal laws in everything you do. Stay away from individuals who may distract you from achieving your goals. Join forces with those who are like minded and can help you achieve your career desires.

Applying these laws in your personal and career circumstances is the secret to your success. The key is to have like-minded people on your support team; people who are also inspired to "**Achieve their Highest Potential**" in their career and lives.

Surrounding yourself with the right group of people will allow you to continue to grow. Your positive energy emerged with their positive energy create an exponential effect allowing each of you to obtain your desired results.

Never forget, always empower your relationships with a view to obtain your desired results like perfect health, and a positive career. As you surround yourself with positive empowering people, they will help you achieve what you set out to achieve, to make adjustments as needed, and push you into a higher level of thinking to achieve your goals.

You also will attract the right mentors that are knowledgeable in your field about what physical and mental attributes you need to acquire. You in turn will inspire other people who are around to follow the good patterns you set in your mind, body, and affairs. This is another way the law of least effort works — bringing to you easily and effortlessly the circumstances and people that will aid you in your success.

Chapter 5
Clear Your Mind of Negative Thoughts Daily

Dr. Gregory Haughton said, *"Freedom from mental captivity means liberating your mind and heart completely from past disappointments, frustration anger and distress."*

The second secret to achieving your highest career potential is to clear your mind daily of negative thoughts, because your negative thoughts are detrimental to your career advancement. Negative thoughts will enter your subconscious mind without you even realizing it. Negative thoughts will sap your mental and physical energy, reduce your level of motivation, and hinder you from achieving your highest career potential.

For instance, negative thoughts based on past negative experiences can increase a person's anxiety, or cause frustration, depression, resentments, anger and even hate. Therefore, make the mental commitment to neutralize all negative thoughts daily before they even enter or worse take root in your subconscious mind.

You should not hold on to negative thoughts for long periods, because your negative thoughts will work against your desire to achieve your career dreams and aspirations.

In fact, the only way you can stay committed to your career goals is to clear your mind of such negative thoughts as: fear, hate, jealousy, greed, anger, pride, etc. daily. The daily radical elimination of negative thoughts will give you dominion over your conscious mind, and will give you the inspiration to stay dedicated to your long term mental commitment and career success.

Your inclination to hold on to negative thoughts will prevent you from reflecting objectively on your daily action plans. To achieve your highest career potential, totally eradicate negative thoughts from your life and career goals. The sooner these thoughts are eradicated from your mind, the stronger, more committed and confident you will become mentally and physically.

To eradicate negative thoughts, reflect daily on your decision making competencies. If you allow negative thoughts to enter your mind, your level of commitment may interfere with your commitment to continue with your daily activities. If problems arise due to your inability to clear your mind of negative thoughts, seek advice and then make the needed mental adjustments as necessary.

To keep negative thoughts from affecting your attitude, emotions and decision making competencies, reflect on your endeavors throughout the day; this will reinforce your mental commitment to your overall career success.

The right mindset will ensure your negative thoughts are objectively addressed; if not addressed your decisions can prevent you from achieving your career goals. Staying abreast with your plan of action requires that you ask yourself these questions daily:

- Am I better at what I did today than yesterday?
- Did I address the things that may have a negative or positive impact on my career growth?
- Am I more disciplined and competent in my decision making skills?
- Am I more knowledgeable in my area of expertise?

Routinely address these questions to uncover unresolved issues which may negatively impact your career path. To gain the maximum results of your mental training, practice these mental exercises routinely, daily is best or at a minimum once per week. This practice will also help to uproot and neutralize negative thoughts. With the right mindset, your dedication, focus and knowledge will improve over time.

On the other hand, positive thoughts will bring an abundance of happiness, wealth, and prosperity if they are allowed to germinate freely. To achieve your highest career potential, meditate only on those positive experiences that can bring forth the best results towards your career goals. Meditation helps to clear negative thoughts and aligns you with your true self and career purpose.

The practice of regular meditation has demonstrated the powerful effects it has on both mind and body.

When you learn to train your mind to focus on positive words and thoughts that are aligned with positive internal energy, it will help you to attract the things you desire. Meditation has helped people align their goals with their actions, which in turn helped them to stay focused and committed to their purpose.

So how does meditation allow you to achieve your highest potential in your career and life? Meditation allows you to connect to your Higher self and cast away unnecessary elements that clutter your consciousness.

Avoid Negative People

Do you entertain and dwell on negative thoughts? Be careful because negative thoughts create negative situations. Decisive people focus their thoughts and feelings on the positive and refrain from thinking any negative thoughts which affect their self-confidence.

Nevertheless, many of us have a terrible time when it comes to avoiding negative conversations and thoughts. If you adopt this important practice of thinking positive thoughts, this right consciousness will enhance your career and personal life; only then will the right mental and physical energy follow. Energy follows thought.

Based on the type of thoughts you emit, your energy will either support you or destroy you.

More importantly, if these negative thoughts enter your mind, they will have a negative impact on your mental and physical preparation and ultimately derail your life plans and goals. It is so important that you are not misled by listening to wrong information or the opinions of others. This is why you should choose positive thoughts and surround yourself with positive and uplifting people so you can maintain high energy to achieve your desired successful results.

Remember that you have dominance over your thoughts; you control your future outcome and career destiny!

Meditate on your words and then speak them into existence and you will grow to appreciate your career decisions. You will advance in your career in a short period of time. You are the gatekeeper of your thoughts, therefore, it is imperative that you learn to clear your mind daily, and maintain the right mindset throughout the day. Therefore, the second secret to achieving your highest career potential is to clear your mind of negative thoughts daily.

Dr. Gregory Haughton

Chapter 6
Cope with Your Success Before It Happens

Dr. Gregory Haughton said, *"Career success should not influence a persons' thoughts, feelings and actions; instead, a persons' thoughts, and actions should positively influence their career success."*

The third secret to achieving your highest career potential is that you practice your career success in your mind before the success actually occurs. Career success and advancement should be handled with grace. As you take on more responsibility with your promotions, make it a point to bring people together and help them achieve their goals as well.

As you achieve your career goals, others may grow to dislike you especially if you demonstrate negative personality traits. In fact, the more successful you become, the more positive your personality traits should be. The more successful you become the more open or receptive you want to become to receiving constructive advice from others, especially your mentors.

Your behavior and attitude towards others should not change in a negative way after you receive a promotion. In fact, if your attitude and mindset demonstrate negative personality traits, you may never attain your promotion or it may be short-lived.

51

Grace is given to the humble, and humiliation to the proud. To grow in your career practice humility! Do everything in your power to stay humble; humility opens new doors that lead to greater success and prosperity. When humility is demonstrated on the job, it shows that you are willing to include and share your success with members of your team.

Humble individuals and leaders are more likely to exude mental and physical confidence and prowess in their abilities when performing their duties and tasks. They are not afraid to empower those around them because they know that it takes a team of successful individuals for long lasting individual and team success.

To avoid mishaps learn to master your emotion, and be extremely knowledgeable in what is expected of you when interacting with people. Successful career individuals spend their time studying in order to understand their mental and physical job responsibilities. They spend even more time in managing their personal weaknesses than their strengths. They maintain a good attitude, work ethic, and they do not allow others to sway them off their course of action.

A major part of your success will depend on whether or not you establish a regular work routine. Successful leaders seldom break their schedule to please anyone. This includes their family or friends.

This means that you don't interrupt your daily schedule of work simply to accommodate others.

Accomplish all important tasks first before you help others. With your priorities aligned, along with the right mindset, you will look and behave differently than everyone else. Your behavior will demonstrate how you are different, exceptional, and are not like everyone else. Practice rigid control, and do not hesitate to give up those things that block your career path to the top.

You may have a strong desire to achieve your career potential, but your career success is best achieved if your activities are narrowed down to the point where your career goals are your primary ambition. You cannot be successful if you create unresolved issues that will distract you from your long term objective.

Make the decision to first control those activities in your life that can be controlled, such as, getting enough sleep so that you can perform your daily duties and responsibilities; eat a balanced meal, which will provide the energy required to think and act according to your short and long term goals; find time to exercise because it will help to relieve your daily mental and physical stress; and communicate daily with your Higher self; just as important, do not take on unnecessary activities that are not related to your career goals.

Having too many things to do that are not aligned with your career goals will only distract you from your primary goal! At times there will be other activities that you desire to do instead of what you know you should be working on, like going to the beach or being with friends or family. Do not give in to these impulses for they very well could sabotage your career. With the right mindset and discipline you can achieve anything you set your mind to.

Do not let outside influences interfere with your quest to achieve your highest career potential. If you focus on one thing you will increase your chances of achieving your highest career potential in less time than you can imagine. This is the third secret to achieving your highest potential -- that you learn to cope with your career success before it actual happens.

Chapter 7
Achieve Your Career Success Now

Dr. Gregory Haughton said, *"Success waits for no man; therefore, commit yourself and start your preparation today; do not wait for tomorrow."*

The fourth secret to achieving your highest potential is that you invest the time and effort to achieve your career success today. Your career success will not happen overnight, but the sooner you begin with your mental preparation, the sooner you will achieve your goal.

Changes can be made only in the now; not yesterday, not tomorrow, next month, nor next year, only today. The power to achieve your highest career potential can only be reached in the now. Purpose in your heart and mind to focus in the now! Staying or living in the past will not help you to achieve your highest career potential. In fact, it prevents you from achieving your highest potential in so many ways.

When you focus on the now, it helps you to manage your work and to guide your actions to achieve your goals. When you stay in the now you have a sense of reality of what is, what is to be and what is to come. For instance, when you are in the now, you set priorities; you plan in advance; you practice on your knowledge and skills and you do everything you can in the now moment to improve in all areas of your career and life.

Once you start living in the now, you will find that achieving your highest career potential is easier than you imagined. All your worries and fears are brought to the surface, so you can then deal with them.

By dealing with the reality of your situation and accepting them for what they are, you give yourself total control of the power you relinquished to your past. Worrying about the past or future is not going to help your current situation; in fact it will only make it worse. So the fourth secret to achieving your highest potential is to focus on the present, because the power lies nowhere else.

Staying or living in the past do you no good. In fact, it prevents you from moving forward in many ways. Instead of focusing on negative thoughts, or on the things you did wrong in the past, focus on more appropriate ways in getting it right today.

Successful people that live in the now, tend to achieve their highest potential easier than those who live in the past. Deal with the reality of your present situation and accept your momentary circumstances for what they are. When you do that you give yourself total control and power to remove any worries, doubts and fears. Worrying about the past or future has never helped anyone's present situation; in fact, it will only make it worse.

Focus On Living your Life in the Now

Do not dwell on past accomplishments too long; stay in the now moment! When I was a young boy becoming a man, I competed for Excelsior High School in Jamaica. While there, I won a lot of medals and trophies.

My mother would hide them, and when I asked her why, she told me that this is not the time to be complacent. She reassured me that what I had accomplished up to that point was an excellent achievement; however, great athletes never become complacent, and don't dwell on past performances.

Being complacent with your past ensures your failure to reach your highest potential in your career, and in your life. It is wise to resolve the past and focus on the present.

As such, be mindful of people who dwell on using the concept of "always" because it is based on the past. "Always" is not based on new or creative energy.

In truth, nothing is ever "always," you may have similar circumstances but they are usually based on different factors which will create different outcomes altogether.

Stay in harmony with your Higher self, and keep your focus in the present, because it is the only point of access to your real power. If you become complacent, you will lose your focus and align with your ego self, the self that was born from what Dr. Davis call your relevant filters of **personal history, personal circumstances and the collective unconscious thoughts of the human race.**

Chapter 8
Your Career Growth Is Most Important

Dr. Gregory Haughton said, *"Physical and mental growth starts with total commitment of mind and body."*

The fifth secret to achieving your highest potential is that your career growth is your number one priority. Most career persons want results to appear overnight, which in most cases is not realistic. For you to improve it takes time, dedication, knowledge and commitment in order to master your duties and responsibilities. In time you will also overcome your weaknesses and develop your strengths in mind and body.

To achieve your highest career potential, focus on longevity and incremental improvements of mind and body! This will give you the time to properly nurture and cultivate your talent and skills. When focusing on longevity and incremental improvements, set realistic goals that are not linked to your ego or pride etc.; stay humble and focus your talent, effort and skills. Always focus on the big picture; your career growth!

The difference between those individuals who achieve their highest career potential and those who fail to achieve their potential is that those who do have developed the right mindset to recognize and also to apply exactly what is required of them. They would then surround themselves with the right people to make it happen.

If you try to take a short cut to achieve your career success then you will only cheat yourself.

Due to the fact that there is a finite time to achieve your highest career potential, devise a plan that gives you the highest probability to succeed. Then implement that plan with great precision!

From time to time evaluate your plan to make sure that your desired results are on track or have been achieved; if it is the outcome you desire, then continue to take the same actions; if not, make the necessary adjustments until you get the results you seek. No drastic changes to your plan should be made at any time because if the course of action is consistent the result will come.

Finally, record your goals daily, because only by tracking your action plan will you be able to visibly identify and see if you are on track to your committed goal. Give considerable thought to the career goals you choose. Make sure that your goals are challenging and rewarding!

Working towards achieving your highest career goals is not a onetime activity, but a habit you establish and continue throughout your career. This is not as complicated as it may appear, and once practiced it will become second nature. In fact we have designed a system that can help all career individuals create a plan based on their talents and their situation.

We know what it feels like to fall short of a career goal. This is why we help individuals to achieve their highest career potential. The fifth secret to achieving your highest career potential is to visualize your growth mentally so it can manifest and understand how important your growth is to your career advancement.

Dr. Gregory Haughton

Chapter 9
Implement the Right Activities to Advance Your Career

Dr. Gregory Haughton said, *"Hard work will not pay dividends when you do the wrong activities."*

The sixth secret to achieving your highest potential is to learn what the right mental and physical activities are in order to get the most out of your hard work and sacrifice. The right mindset, desires and motivation are enough to guide you on your path to know the most suitable type of mental and physical activities that best suit your career advancement.

The right mindset will inspire you to work smart by doing the right physical and mental activities that will advance your career aspirations.

When the purpose has been set in your mind to excel by doing the right activities, you will no longer need to worry about compromising your career longevity for quick success.

With a real intent in your mind to advance your career, your desire will inspire you to reach out to work with successful career professionals and experts; these experts have the knowledge and experience to take you to where you need to be.

Never doubt your ability to move up and advance in your career. As a matter of fact, opportunities will present themselves for you to perform duties that are outside your job description but will make a lasting impression on your superiors. Take advantage of these opportunities to demonstrate your capabilities and willingness to go the extra mile.

If you devote your time to doing the right activities, it will increase your confidence in your ability to perform at your highest potential and as a result, it will bring out the best in you in and out of the workplace setting.

The right mindset will remind you that working harder every day is not necessarily the best strategy to advance your career goals; but that even more important is doing the right activities. Those who work the hardest are not always the most successful. In fact, the hardest working individuals who are not doing the right activities become burnt out or depressed before they have a chance at the promotion they desire.

Doing the right activities will help you to improve gradually in your area of expertise without putting unnecessary wear and tear on your mind and body. To achieve your highest career potential make sure that your mind is strong enough to support your physical activities and commitments.

Be mentally vested in everything that goes on in and around you. To achieve your highest career potential, you need to not only do the physical training, which is only 20% of your career success, but place extreme focus on the 80% which is the mental preparation. Spend more time focusing on implementing powerful strategies, and the proper execution of your career duties and responsibilities.

To achieve your highest career potential follow intelligent and sensible rules, guidelines and principles. You'll need to work on your strong points, but practice especially hard on your weak points. In fact, work twice as hard to improve your weak points as you do on your strengths. By doing this you'll make yourself more complete and balanced with little or no vulnerabilities. The sixth secret to achieving your highest potential is doing the right type of physical activities or practices.

Dr. Gregory Haughton

Chapter 10
The Right Fuel for Your Body and Mind

Gregory Haughton once said, *"Those who truly respect their body and mind will not fuel it with junk foods as their main source of energy."*

The final secret to achieving your highest career potential is having and following the right nutritional plan. It is almost impossible to have a long and lasting career without eating the appropriate foods required to nourish the body and mind. If you are to achieve your highest career potential then you need to research and work closely with experts that can guide you in choosing a dietary plan that best suits your individual need.

Without the right diet you won't have the energy to push your mind and body to the limit. With the right diet at the most opportune time, your body will adapt to the physical stress, the wear and tear to your muscles, joints, ligaments and tendons.

This brings about stability, consistency and longevity in your career. With the right diet and supplementation plan, your body will be able to repair, rebuild and cleanse itself in a timely manner. This is where the true power of physical improvement lies.

Additionally, eat three meals a day. It is best to prepare your meals in advance and take them with you. Avoid eating unnecessary junk foods. These will only create excessive waste and mucus buildup in your system.

Proper Nourishment

One of the biggest challenges we face today is what is the proper food to eat without compromising our health? The misinformation about eating is detrimental to the health and longevity of not only athletes but individuals as well.

It might seem hard to believe, but most of the foods we consume have little or no nutritional value; it only produces a lot of waste in our system. If this waste is not removed quickly, the body becomes toxic, which leads to imbalances in our immune system.

When it comes to proper eating habits, such as when, why and how to eat, most of us make our decisions based on tradition, customs and convenience. We don't realize that our body is a system that is governed by physical laws. Over time, as we continue to ignore these laws our health and longevity is compromised.

When we refuse to obey the laws of a proper nourishing diet this causes our body and its digestive system to slowly deteriorate resulting in various illnesses.

The consequences of a poor diet are usually not instantaneously evident so we don't connect the dots.
Proper digestion is about nourishing the entire body and not just getting food in and out of the body to please our appetites. Avoid eating the wrong food combinations because it will cause fermentation, which creates unnecessary complications in your digestive system. The body must be able to absorb and assimilate the nutrients we ingest in order to create and repair the cells.

Original and natural seed-yielding food sources are considered healthy and best for your body. Examples of these food types include apples, avocados, grapes, watermelon, tomatoes etc. as they do not leave a lot of waste in the body when consumed.

When we choose to eat natural and fresh fruits and vegetables, we do not invite medical challenges, sickness and diseases in our lives. In order to overcome these medical challenges, there are some basic things we should be aware of to keep our body systems functioning well. Eating healthy food is a lifelong endeavor; everything we eat should assist in extending our health and longevity.

To obtain optimal health, seek guidance from experienced professionals who can educate you on how to best take care of your body. Never take the gift of life for granted! Do the right things for your body and you will be richly blessed!

As we look at the art and science of eating and digestion, it is imperative that we understand how the body works with regards to how the food we eat affects our entire body systems and its' functions.

As a society our eating concepts are wrong, hence, we are plagued with numerous health problems such as heart attacks, strokes, diabetes, arthritis, high blood pressure, colon problem, etc. and the most ruthless of them all - cancer.

A major mistaken notion is that breakfast is not only the most important meal of the day but that it should be largest meal.
Eating the wrong types of food for breakfast is one of the worst things you can do to your body. Why do I say that? Many of us were taught that when we eat a large breakfast it will give us the necessary energy for our daily physical and mental activities. This is absolutely not true!

When we eat a large breakfast, it always leads to improper digestion. We actually clog our system by pushing waste back into our tissues and cells, causing toxins to settle in our bloodstream. What are toxins? Toxins are any poisonous substances produced by the cells or organisms in our body.

With improper digestion along with high levels of stress, and pollution, we continuously create and release toxins into our body.

Pollutions come from the chemicals we breathe in from the air, from the water we drink, and from the foods we eat. If these toxins are not flushed out of the body regularly with the right type of foods, the accumulation of toxins in the body overtime can eventually manifest as disorders or illnesses.

Let's pretend that your body is a car, and the manufacture's instructional manual clearly states that you should change your engine oil every 2-3 months or every 3000 miles. Then imagine driving your car for more than 3 years without getting an oil change or a tune up. I promise you that within that time period your check engine light will come on, your engine and transmission fuel will be low or all gone, your windshield wiper fuel will be empty and any other number of car problems will occur.

Our body operates just like a motor vehicle; but unlike a motor vehicle that is unable to take care of itself, we have the option of taking good care of our bodies. We are given warning signals that we should adhere to and act upon but many of us ignore them. A few of these signals appear as headaches, stiff joints, unpleasant body odor, feeling dull and sleepy after eating, dizziness, feeling tired, experiencing aches, pains, and constipation.

When we ignore and don't act on these signals this can result in major illnesses such as cancer, strokes and other serious health problems. This is further complicated by a health care system which treats only the symptoms and not the cause itself. Therefore it behooves you to educate yourself!

There are three distinct phases to observe that our body experiences within a 24-hour period. These phases are divided into three eight hour periods. These are called the Sleep – Mini Fast Phase, the Elimination – Breakfast Phase, and the Intake – Between Lunch and Dinner Phase.

Sleep – Mini Fast Phase

The most critical eight hour phase is when we sleep. Since we are unable to eat during this eight hour period the body experiences a mini fast.

During this phase the body is breaking down old or dead cells, rebuilding new cells and doing what it can to heal and regenerate your body.

By the end of this mini fast or by the time you wake up in the morning, there are a lot of dead cells or toxins that the body now needs to remove from the system and/or bloodstream.

If these toxins are not removed before you consume a highly concentrated protein or carbohydrate meal, you will add more toxins and wastes into your body and you will begin to feel lethargic, hungry, sleepy etc.

Breakfast - the Elimination Phase

In the second eight hour period, the body automatically goes into the elimination mode, and attempts to get rid of, or move out any waste that was generated from the day before, or during the sleep-mini fast phase. During this time period ingest specific types of food that will assist your body to properly eliminate built up toxins and waste.

The original intent and meaning of the English word "Breakfast" was to break a fast (the sleep -mini fast phase) as the first meal of the day. This is how the concept of breakfast began.

The best way to break a fast is with liquids and fruits. I normally start the morning with a glass of room temperature water. Throughout the morning up until early afternoon I drink herbal teas, naturally made plant based milk, natural fruit and/or vegetable juices.

If you understand the purpose of fasting you understand that breaking the fast is as important as the fast itself. Science shows that when you fast the stomach shrinks according to the amount of waste that is emptied of your prior day's consumed food.

As we break this mini fast we need to open up the stomach to its original size. We need to clean out the entire digestive system which is done by eating or ingesting specific types of food.

When this is done properly we open the stomach slowly and gradually so that the body can adjust to the elimination of this waste.

Unfortunately, the way most of us break our fast these days causes more harm than good. The food that we generally eat in the morning is not good for cleansing out wastes and toxins and therefore is not the appropriate type of food required to break a fast.

When we break our fast incorrectly in the morning with the wrong types of foods such as (breakfast cereal, eggs, sausages, donuts, etc.), what actually happens is that the waste that was released the night before is pushed back into the cells and tissues. As such the waste and toxins continue to build up in our body.

This is the reason so many are suffering from obesity, diabetes, high blood pressure, cancer and other types of cardiovascular diseases. When the body is so overwhelmed with waste, we may feel tired and sluggish when we get up in the morning.

The Intake Phase – Between Lunch and Dinner

The third eight hour period is the intake phase which is between lunch and dinner. This is the time to consume our protein, fat and carbohydrates. However, 20 percent

74

raw vegetables should be consume when eating protein, fat and carbohydrates. The best protein to eat daily is a variety of beans (Black, red, kidney, soy etc.).

Proteins, carbohydrates and concentrated rich foods are low in minerals which the body needs in order to properly process the food we eat. Keep in mind that when we eat meat or other types of proteins, it requires an acid medium, which are specific enzymes found in the intestines for breaking down meat.

Carbohydrates such as potatoes, yam, rice etc. require an alkaline enzyme for digestion. When we eat carbohydrates and protein at the same time, the body is not able to secrete both digestive juices simultaneously in response to the incoming protein and starch. This promptly neutralizes (cancels out) one another, leaving a weak watery solution in the stomach, causing the carbohydrate to ferment in the stomach.

If the carbohydrates are undigested they do not to turn into sugar, which in turn ferments and turns into alcohol. This putrefaction and fermentation is the primary cause of digestive distress, including gas, heartburn, cramps, bloating, constipation, foul stool bleeding piles and the list goes on. Try to eat carbohydrates that are green leafy vegetables because these will absorb the sugar and release it at a slower pace into the blood stream.

When this happens, the body is better able to burn and utilize the sugar which will provide one with more energy throughout the day.

Drink plenty of water to keep your body hydrated. Physical and mental burnouts are caused by not having enough electrolytes and fluids in the system.

Having the right diet and nutritional plan is so important that I was compelled to design a step by step formula to help you to eat and take the right supplements at the right time. I will show you what to eat and what supplements to take before, during and after work. This plan will meet your individual needs – I guarantee it.
The seventh secret to achieving your highest potential is to have the right diet and supplementation plan.

Conclusion

I would like to say thank you for taking the time to purchase this book. It is our desire to provide you with the important tools to assist you in being the best person you can be. Too often, employees are denied a successful career because they do not have the competencies or the knowledge to carefully think through the process of career advancement on their own.

To improve your knowledge and competencies in your career, mentorship is extremely useful in guiding your thoughts and actions especially during the preliminary stages of your career.

Employees, who understand the causes for their career mistakes or failures, can quickly learn to recognize the deficiencies of their previous decision making skills and can make the modifications necessary to improve in their areas of weakness.

On several occasions, I mentioned the concept of "Everything starts in the mind first." In light of all that you do, you are only truly competing with your former and current self.

As such, winning is based on your determination to convince yourself that you will stick to a game plan regardless of how you feel.

What this means is that whenever you perform, your execution is always independent of your opponents, thus, your mindset will determine your future career outcome. By the same token, a weak mind is defined in the same way. Be true and honest with yourself and ask, "Did I execute everything fully today?" "Did I truly do my very best today?" If either answer is no, then for you, a weak mindset determined that day.

Remember, to achieve your highest career potential, change the way you think. We know that success begins in the mind. If you follow the foundational information in this book, your time was spent wisely. In the future your energy will not be wasted and you will avoid the effort of putting unnecessary wear and tear on your body and mind.

We have focused our efforts on providing valuable information that will assist you to make better informed decisions, make your professional career easier, less stressful and more manageable.

Unfortunately, the type of mindset that you need to really advance your career quickly is difficult to explain in a book. This is why the most successful people have mentors. In the next section I will explain how we can assist you in reaching your highest career potential.

Here is What I Have for You

Haughton Mentoring Program

The Haughton Mentoring Group and Dr. Haughton have mentored numerous career individuals to achieve great career and personal success. Career individuals who have received mentoring in our program have experienced more positive outcomes in their career than those who were not mentored.

Our mentoring programs enhanced our mentees' self-image and psychological well-being. Most of our mentees reported greater success, and higher engagement over problem-focused coping behavior. They are more likely to seek support when encountering problems and drawbacks.

As your mentor we will create an environment where your learning is combined with your personal knowledge and experience. We also provide the psychosocial support to develop your cognitive knowledge and skills. As your cognitive knowledge and skills increase through our interactions, you will be able to implement steps or a sequence of behaviors to help you achieve your tasks. Our program will increase your declarative, strategic, and tactical knowledge (factual and theoretical insights) through conversations, and other forms of interactions during our sessions.

You will receive benefits in the form of emotional, career, and psychosocial support. We are aware that most mentees have different needs; however, the objectives will always be the same; to achieve your desired professional and career goals.

Most mentees desire emotional and psychosocial support during our interaction. We ensure that emotional and psychosocial support is extended to you in the forms of acceptance, counseling, coaching, and friendship.

Our program has helped mentees to develop:
- A professional identity
- Personal competence
- Moral outlook
- Leadership capabilities
- A high level of confidence
- Increased risk-taking capacities

Haughton Mentoring online programs are web-based courses, and live seminars designed to create an interesting, interactive learning environment. Our mentoring educational virtual classroom is comfortable. You can take our mentoring courses or watch our live seminars at your convenience as long as you have access to the World Wide Web. Lesson plans, are posted online; while individuals/mentors interact while live streaming over the Internet.

Scheduled discussions, email messages, live chats and real-time group discussions are a few of the opportunities for interacting during our mentoring courses. You will also have access to online career advice and technical support via email or telephone.

Before enrolling in an online course, we encourage you take watch our free introductory videos and also take our Free Mental evaluation and view the Demo Course to see if our online mentoring fits your learning style and current plans.

Our career mentoring programs are designed to enhance organizational advancement through individual mentoring, which will help you develop the poise and confidence necessary to achieve your full potential in your career at the highest level.

The mentoring methodology that we use empowers individuals to reinvent themselves by becoming more consciously aware of their frames of reference, behaviors and thinking. This is most successful when performed in a positive, nurturing environment, which we provide.

We provide a support mechanism structured to promote your mental and psychological career development. As a part of our individualized mentoring program, we provide you with the education, training, and emotional support you need to achieve your highest potential.

How You Will Benefit by Working with a HMG Mentor:

- Begin to manage your time and energy wisely; do more work with less time.
- Create your own **personal career goals and strategies**.
- **Understand the difference between working hard and working smart**.
- Learn how to measure and track your career performance.
- Discover how to build alliances and ensure your career growth.
- Identify **key management and personnel to help you advance in your career goals.**

Remember, to achieve your highest career potential, change the way you think! Top executives do not simply reach the top by working hard alone. Instead, they get the mentoring necessary to take control of and succeed in their career. No matter how challenging or competitive your workplace environment, you can learn to advance and maximize your potential with our mentoring program. If you are looking for more support in implementing the teachings in this book let a HMG mentors help you develop a plan to succeed in your current career.

Here Is What I Want You to Do Next

Special Offer: To help you achieve your career potential, subscribe to receive our new guide of "SECRETS TO HAVING A SUCCESSFUL CAREER" immediately when you sign-up for a FREE introduction to HMG. Your decision to read this book will change your life, but don't stop now because our next book will give you a step by approach to increasing your career and personal life.

Dr. Gregory Haughton

NOTES